A WORLD ONCE KNOWN

A WORLD ONCE KNOWN

Al Zolynas

©2024 by Al Zolynas, all rights reserved

ISBN: 979-8-9858194-8-9

A World Once Known was published in Brooklyn, New York, on March 1, 2024 by Black Spruce Press.
Design by Regina Schroeder
Cover photograph "Tropical Reverie" © Spencer McWilliams

Black Spruce Press.org
BlackSprucePress@gmail.com
Manufactured in the United States of America

ACKNOWLEDGEMENTS

Grateful acknowledgement is made to the following publications, in which some of these poems have appeared: *An Activists' Poetry Anthology: Selected Poems for Good Trouble; Australian Poetry 1988; The Big Toe Review; Canard Anthology: City Works Anthology; The Death of Beans; Lithuania: In Her Own Words— An Anthology of Contemporary Lithuanian Writing; Lituanus; Minnesota Poetry Outloud; Nueva Poesia de Los Angeles; Poem Hunter; Poetry Now; Portfolio; Quadrant; San Diego Poetry Annual; Steelhead 5.*

For Arlie, as always.

CONTENTS

I.

II.

III.

I.

The Would-Be Painter

On days like this, when I've risen early and invited
the Muse and she, despite my pleadings, continues
to sleep and won't be roused, and I've stared
into the blank page
and heard my life ticking away,
I think about switching genres, nay, media...nay,
art forms. I'll just give up words,
I say to myself; I'll show 'em, I'll take up...
painting. Yes, I'll become a painter!

I can see me now in my studio,
a wide open capacious space
above the waves,
the whole place bathed in Northern Light
(it must be Northern Light), me standing
in front of a canvas the size of a movie screen
with step-ladders and scaffolding when I need them.

I'm surrounded by scores of canvases
in various stages of completion—
landscapes, still-lifes, nudes, abstracts in all the styles:
impressionistic, expressionistic, realistic, etc.
(You know the list)...Why, there's that super-
realistic still-life I did
of a human pelvic bone encircling a ripe anjou pear,
and those cubist and pointillist pieces from my early period
(alas, they never sold years ago, and now I won't part
with them out of sheer curmudgeonliness).

I think I see an assistant in the corner...yes, I do.
I must confess she's a young, nubile beauty in a short robe
who doubles as my model. She's stirring
a can of acrylic paint or making us cappuccinos.
Her name is...Helène and she's from...

Arles, yes, Arles, France...and she's on special scholarship
paid for by the École des Beaux Arts,
come all this way to apprentice
with the world master. Yes, it's true,
I'm a famous painter, but fame has not ruined me;

I continue to dedicate my entire life
to the furthering of my Art, everyone's Art, pushing
out the boundaries with fierce commitment but with grace
and humor as well. I'm respected, revered and, yes,
I must say it, loved. The Art World is abuzz
before each of my new shows:
What will X boggle us with next?
What gauntlet will X throw down this time?
How many lesser painters will finally
throw in their brushes and air guns in despair?

I'm constantly expanding the boundaries.
My current project focuses on merging media:
the canvas I'm in front of, the one
I told you was as large as a movie screen?
Well, it is a movie screen and even now a movie
is playing on it, projected from behind.
My technique has progressed to such a degree
I can paint the movie as it is being shown!

This requires my focused concentration as well
as the full engagement of my body and soul.
I must at the same time be a dancer and a shaman.
At the end of your typical ninety-minute movie
I'm sweating like a prize-fighter; I'm tired,
but fulfilled, at least momentarily, for I have rendered
a movie on canvas (not captured, no, not that!).
Anyone looking at my moviepainting
will no longer be the same person.

Such is the technique, the power, the sheer
transformative miracle of my Art. My next project
will be to shoot a movie, paint the movie
while filming myself painting, this on commission
from the Bravo channel. After that, I'll be ready
for my ultimate project. Already, I'm deeply involved
in preparations, working out every day,
drinking many cups of cappuccino and researching
quantum physics and the latest Theory of Everything:
I will engage in nothing less than painting,
as it occurs, the moving world!

Trying To Save An Insect

Taking out the trash, I almost step on him. Black beetle struggling along. Dragging himself across the pitted cement path. I put my sack down. He seems to be wearing some kind of a gray sweater knitted out of miniature wool. Suddenly, he flips over on his back. I see five of his six legs tangled up in spider web. Struggling to free himself, he waves them about awkwardly like a baby in a crib trapped among knotted skeins of wool.

I go inside, get my reading glasses, my tiniest pair of scissors, the ones I use to trim nose hair. Carefully, I cut as much of the web away from his legs as I can, though they're still encased in miniature gray leggings and socks. The clotted web on his back I can't free without risking damage to his carapaced wing protectors. I have no choice but to leave him with his little sweater on. At least he can crawl again, which he now does in a straight line, full of purpose, as it seems to me, across the path with not even a backward glance and into the shadows of the ground cover.

Landscape With Figures And Train

Imagine a train on its way from Sydney to Melbourne
somewhere in New South Wales
in the middle of a stifling summer
(this is before diesel engines, before air conditioning),
the smoke and soot from the locomotive pouring into carriages
through open windows. See there also
a family of four sitting in their cubicle
enduring the long sweaty hours
playing cards or chess or staring trance-like
at the bleak landscape as it undulates
in ancient waves beneath them.

Somewhere near Wagga Wagga
imagine the train slows unaccountably,
and the boy of the family
looks up from the chessboard
and is face to face
with a solitary Aboriginal, a man,
virtually naked, standing as if planted
in the dusty earth
not more than a dozen paces from the train's open window.
Tall and thin, he stands on one leg, his other foot
resting on his inner knee
(just as depicted in the grainy black and white
photographs in the Australian Junior Encyclopedia
which sits next to the Arthur Mee's on the boy's
bedroom desk in Sydney).
The man is holding and leaning on a spear.
Imagine the train moving slowly, the boy
noticing that the Aboriginal stares straight ahead,
not at the train but through it as if
it were a momentary interruption in the landscape.

Years later the boy, as a young man
on another continent, learns
of the notion of the Noble Savage,
and at that moment, while others see
Sioux or Cheyenne or Apache, he sees
the Aboriginal standing alone in front of him.
Later, he also learns of the unreliability of memory—
even of history itself,
its distortions, agendas, and self-serving inventions.
Finally, imagine, too, that the boy—then and now—
unaccountably, would give almost anything
to return to that hot day,
to see the world through that man's eyes,
to feel it through the soles of his feet.

The Gift At Dove Cottage, A Sonnet

He stole a moment in William Wordsworth's chair,
adjusted his arms, firmly planted his feet,
imagined two women there—at his feet—
ready to take down his words. Nowhere
else had he felt so charged, as though his hair
were myriad antennae catching the heat
of Creation itself. And iambs, replete
with images and metaphors, were there,
and Pentameter, like a mythic snake
beneath the ever-warming morning sun,
came alive, pulsed. He felt he'd won
a moment in some other realm, or that Grace
gave out for Wordsworth's, for Poetry's sake
to him for a time in that shadow-crowded place.

The Worn, The Used

Something in the worn and used,
the torn and abused, something
we love and seek and are comforted by,
something soulful...

The things we use over and over,
handle unconsciously through the hours and days—
the leather wallets gleaming softly and sadly
their rubbed and worn patinas
as we split them open like ripe fruit:
Here, World, a little something for You in gratitude
for all Your gifts...or a bribe against
the fear of pain...

How a boy's new shoes need immediate scuffing,
to be stomped through puddles, soiled, mud-caked,
despite a mother's horror...

Headwear—hats, caps, baseball, fedoras,
the best ones sweat-stained along rim and bill,
thumb-worn where we've reached
over and over for the necessary adjustment...

And blue jeans—a whole modern industry born
from marketing the "pre-worn" versions,
the purchased good use,
false substitute for the real,
all those hours of uncomfortable wear by-passed
while that magic fabric "de Nîmes"
slowly faded, released
its inky blue, conformed to the body's shape,
snug in the crotch for those certain few
who can pull off their brazen self-revelations...

Even this little notebook—how
I take pride in its slow wear as it bends
to a curve hugging my left buttock, how
the edges fray, how the cover
becomes more and more pitted...

Good tools—the hammer's smooth handle,
the well-sharpened kitchen knife,
the bright silver arc of the shovel's edge...

Those cotton T-shirts worn only at home,
moving more and more towards transparency
with each wash, how soft they are, how
pleasing their lightness on our shoulders...

Now, in front of me in the waiting room, that pink
canvas bag, slightly stained, corner-worn,
bottom-grimed, fumbled in
by the Millenial teenager
with her pink and black hair, sexy
in her designer jeans.
She's chic, but not too,
not slick, plastic, like so much
in our disposable world...

Have we entered into some kind
of secret compact with entropy itself?
Even as "things fall apart," what is it that watches and
relishes our solidarity
with all the beautiful disappearances?

Apple on A Desk

You call my attention away
from routine papers, your red and yellow
presence in afternoon light, your
round and silent pregnancy.
Little globe of sweet juice and pulp,
I see now your bruise badges,
your encounters with the world's rough edges.
How the light holds you round and singular,
your curved stem like a hangnail,
out of place, or like
the black wick of a cartoon bomb.
You won't explode, though, not again, not
beyond the big bang of your being, your
inexpressible sweet presence
here on my desk, both of us
both changing and unchanging
as the light carries
and holds us in this afternoon.

Incident Outside A Café

I'm sipping espresso outside among
the mumble and jumble of my fellow humans,
the comings and goings of errand runners,
late morning shoppers
and coffee break takers.

A crow and a seagull engage each other
in the parking lot—
Black Crow on black tarmac is trying
to pry up a flattened, stale hamburger bun.
White Seagull, yellow-legged and yellow-eyed,
hops up and down, rides the air just above him,
swoops down on Hopkins' wimpling wing,
squawks and carries on.

But it's no go for Seagull; Crow has dibs,
shielding his find with black shoulders.
Seagull, who's a good ten miles from the coast,
Finally concedes Crow's inland claims,
arcs up on a couple of wing beats
and with a parting plaintive cry catches
the westward wind in a long glide.
Crow caws his way up an air ladder
and lights on a eucalyptus branch
thirty feet above us all.

The parking lot on this mid-week chilly day
returns to its dour functionality,
we humans easing in and out of our vehicles,
self-absorbed, lost under the autumn sky,
under Crow's watchful eye.

Night Watch

It is the summer of 1953, three o'clock in the morning
somewhere near Ingleburn
above the Georges River, half-way
through the third two-hour night watch.

Two boys—twelve and eight—are guarding
a sleeping camp full of scouts.
In the center of the cleared compound
a bare flagpole points to the Milky Way,
its two flags, Australian and Lithuanian, both
folded away for the night in the camp master's tent.
There, too, rest a portable typewriter and stencil machine
for preparing the camp's daily newsletter.
Near the pillows of sleeping boys and girls
lie scouting handbooks
written in Lithuanian, originally printed in Lithuania, now
reprinted in Marrickville.
They contain numerous references to flora and fauna:
linden and birch trees, rue flowers, elk and wolf that
you could spend three lifetimes searching for
around Ingleburn and never find.
The boys and girls have been required
to memorize large sections of the Handbook.
There will be Tests.

The two boy-guards walk quietly
back and forth across the compound,
occasionally shining their torches
into the surrounding bush, not so much
because of some possible threat,
but to see the pale beams of light
pierce the dark;
they shine them, too, straight up at the stars
and arc them back and forth across each other
in a silent sword fight of dueling light.

Around them the tall gums loom,
the only sound the crackle of the fire
and the crystal ping of vermillion coals
falling in on themselves.
The boys are alert to the deep silence of the night.
The younger one has never been up this late,
never been given the responsibility of Night Watch.
But they are boys and soon grow bored with deep silences.
In a whisper, the twelve year-old challenges the eight year-old
to leap over the campfire.

For the next twenty minutes they sprint
from the dark edge of the compound
silently and swiftly and jump over the dwindling fire, over
the momentary blast of heat,
again and again.
No one wakes as their shadows
swirl along the circle of tents,
leap through the trees and up among the stars.

For The Dunny Man, Around 1954

When we lived in a rented garage
on Clark Street in Bass Hill,
the Dunny Man came once each week
to haul away our full cans.
He always worked fast,
the driver of the truck also, roaring
and clattering down our unpaved street,
slamming to a halt in front of the house
in a cloud of dust and flies.

He was a small, wiry man,
shirtless, in stained and torn khaki shorts
and cracked hobnailed infantry boots
that had probably gotten him through
the jungles of New Guinea or the deserts of North Africa
and God knows what horrors.

He wore broad, bat-winged leather shoulder pads
supported by straps crossing his chest like bandoleers,
an alien creature right out of a Saturday matinee—
alien except for an all too human face.

Onto his shoulders he'd hoist up
a week's worth of our shit and piss,
and with a "G'day, Mate" wink his squinty eye at me,
cigarette-end stuck in the corner of his mouth,
and bandy legs working like pistons,
he'd quick-march
the sloshing stuff back to the truck,
staggering under the load.

When our family moved to the new fibro house
in Bankstown, the one my father built
with his own urgent, Displaced Person's hands,

we finally had our own indoor toilet,
its pale-green porcelain commode
flushing as sweetly as any rill in a secluded glen,

and the Dunny Man vanished, went the way
of the Horse and Cart Milkman, and Breadman,
the Man Who Peddled Clothesline Poles,
the Door-to-Door Knife and Scissors Sharpener,
and the Man Who Delivered Cola in Stoneware Jugs—
all sucked into the vacuum trailing progress.

I think of the Dunny Man now
and see those boots and hear the hobnails
on the concrete path, and the thin legs, the knotted
calves, his body bent sideways, leaning out
under the heavy cans, under
the weight of all that stinking human waste,
he the archetypal Aussie battler who could take
whatever life dished out, and took it
and took it some more.

Fingers

most distant and most intimate
furthest from the center
closest to the world
tendrils, tentacles of touch
dactylions of delight

we're pickers and stealers for sure
hookers and pointers
master manipulators, players
and grabbers, prodders and feelers
we palpate and poke the world

on their behalf
scratch their itches, pick
and thumb their noses
run amok over their guitars and pianos
wear their gaudy rings

button and unbutton, zip
and unzip their clothes
drum their impatience
gesticulate their frustration
smooth down their children's hair

make the claw
make the fist
make the karate chop
make the handshake
make the open-palmed gesture of giving

crash together in the clap
come together silently
in the prayer, the "namaste"
the greeting
the parting

Fifth Day, Sesshin

sipping tea during a rest break
eyes lowered
someone walks past in sandaled feet
those feet right then
one foot really
one step
one part of one step
heel rising
foot poised then
rolling forward onto ball and toes
that moment
that instant
there was nothing
else and
whatever that was
was all of it
simply
all of it

[*Sesshin:* Japanese, a Zen multi-day meditation retreat]

Triage

(in split voice—earnest, hysterical, tired)

Hey, first things first!
Seven point nine billion plus on the planet; we got to get food
and clothing to them all...
> (Right after this cup of coffee, man, we begin the program,
> the reform, we implement the radical transformation, get
> the transworld electric grid set up, power for all).

Hey, I say, first things first!
The ozone's going, there's a hole in the sky, we got to plug it,
man!...
> (Right after this second cup, we get that international
> conference in place,
> get the delegates flying in from all corners, the shakers and
> movers, the big science guys, the politicos...).

Hey, let's stay focused—first things first!
The world's bleeding, the trees are dropping, screaming in an
agony of wood chips, severed vines, a flutter of parrots caught
in air, no place to land, a fragmented disappearing rainbow of
feathers...
> (As soon as we get out of this committee meeting on
> planning and future implementation, as soon as we've
> elected the new members from the old membership and
> approved the minutes of the last meeting—assuming we
> have a quorum today...uh, do we?).

I say, again, to you, to myself, first things first!
Bring me more bandages, compresses, a heart-lung machine, a
kidney dialysis machine! We're desperate! This is serious, man;
we may not make it...It's so hot!
> (O.K., O. K., let me just answer these few dozen emails that
> just now came in over the cyber transom; it won't take me
> more than the rest of the morning. Don't worry, I can trash
> 85% of them unread)..

First things first...please?...
        (Lunch? It's lunch time already?
        Let's get back together
        right after lunch, O. K.?)

Hamlet On The Planet

I've heard that, night or day, twenty-four-seven,
as the Millenials would say, Hamlet
struts his stuff, somewhere on the stages of
this world, this-our dear planet, this blessèd
plot, this earth, this realm, this England...oops, beg
your pardon, right rhythm, wrong play...somewhere

even now, for the umpteenth time, in theaters,
real and virtual, on videos, D
VDs, Hamlet works through endless cycles
of grief and the blues, through his abuses
at the hands of fate and his cruel uncle,
through his own too sallied, sullied, solid,
soiled, or sordid flesh...procrastination—
if that's what it is—and his anger and
suicidal thoughts, the self-perceived short-
comings of his own tragic character.

At last estimate, eight billion of us
crowd this jungle-thinned, ozone-depleted,
ocean-polluted one-world-space-ship-earth-
archipelago-global-village, our
dear home, our crapped-in nest, the only place
we know and presumably love though can't
seem to take care of with liberty, justice,
and sustainability for all...Ah,
'tis a wish devoutly to be desired!

Somewhere, e'en now, the dark prince of Denmark,
the put-upon, suffering son of a dear
father fowly murthered, reminds us that
though we jig and amble it will come to
this, this rest which is silence...and therefore
would it not be good for us to come to
before forced to it at the point of a
dagger, foil, dirk, snee, or bare bodkin, yes?

Moonlight/Moonshade

After watching a chunk of "The Big Sleep,"
that is, listening to it and using the blurred images
for eye exercises, and having the occasional flash of clear vision
(Bogey's hand striking a match, lighting a cigarette,
Bacall's beautiful angular face), I turn off the tv
with the remote control,
kill the lights and prepare for bed.

In the kitchen I notice the moonlight,
soft and friendly towards my myopia,
somehow undiminished by it.
In fact, this moonlight seems more real now
than any memory of the sun's hard edges and clear planes.
The moonlight caresses the dishes in the drainer, the sink;
it dimly gleams off fixtures and mists the floor
into which my phosphorescent bare feet wade now.
I am like a man waking in a dream
to find himself fording a stream
in the middle of a forest in the middle of the night,
lost, somehow, and happy.

Note To Self: Don't Burn Your Poems

they aren't yours anyway

the ones destined for some longevity
will survive despite your efforts

the ones not
will filter away
or lie dreaming vaguely in the limbo
of the library's Special Collection

or perhaps in some poetry lover's
imperfect memory

Wrists

In the deep of night they ache, curled
in upon themselves,
autumn leaves in slow-motion
centripetal spiral
towards winter and the inner dark,
curling in sleep toward the heart,
the body folding in on itself,
fruitless attempt
at self-protection.
Sometimes,
in half-sleep, they straighten, open
like painful hinges on the dark,
and in that floating half-dream, live
for a moment
unprotected,
open to the night
and its silent stars.

Flags, Outside The Aboriginal Museum, Huskisson, New South Wales

The new Aboriginal flag—round yellow sun
against black and red earth
and sky—stands straight out
from its pole, picked up and held for a moment
by the wind, as if
by a gentle hand.

Next to it, the old national flag—Union
Jack, Southern Cross, blue empyrean field,
the sum total of its majesty
hidden in folds of cloth—hangs limply,
a mottled rag, dead in a pocket of still air.

That's how it is with flags.
In the end, much depends on the wind,
its direction, how it blows.

Gifts

They all came together briefly,
the things we thought
could make us happy:
sunlight and clouds,
delicious food,
a loving companion, a transparent river
with floating ducks and foot-long trout,
a stone bridge with passers-by
leaning on elbows,
gazing down into water,
an ancient stone church
complete with quarter-hour tolling
bell, even a graveyard with its famous
remains of a 19th century poet.
We sat above the river
on a summer's noon, eating, talking the talk
of travelers, feeding sparrows and wrens bold enough
to hop onto our table, even the edges of our plates,
to present us with the intimacy of feathers,
the perfection of their feet, their intelligent eyes.
Our waitress, a tall sixteen-year old
blond with rosy cheeks, wore a silver stud
in one nostril and an expression of pure
teenaged resentment,
her own astonishingly beautiful face darkened,
eyes clouded, unaware,
at least at that moment of her own beauty,
the beauty around her.
I imagined her thoughts were on the day
when she could leave this place,
head south, set herself up in London.
Did she hear the bell ringing out
its two-sided message?
Time is running out.

There is no time.
Time is running out.
There is no time.

26

Summer, The Lake District

Walking In Morning Rain

Little flotillas of snails
are crossing the sidewalk, sailing slowly
from one green sward to another.
What gets them moving?
Blind instinct? (whatever that is).
Though the green fields are as equal
as the two sides of an equation,
the snails are leaving
one just as much as the other.
A simple case of the "grass is greener"?
Is the flat and cool concrete
with its skin of moving water
a relief from the tight
forests of green blades?
And why, for that matter, do snails come out
mostly in rain? To stop from drowning?
To celebrate? To mate? The scientist in me
wants to know, but something deeper
knows all "whys"
lead nowhere, and also perhaps
guides my steps—two miles out
and two miles back—keeps my eyes scanning
the path in front,
and somehow puts
my feet down where there are
no snails.

At The Carwash

Ablaze in his new red and gold Mr. Sudz T-shirt,
the young migrant, miles
from the pueblo of his birth,
twirls a damp red wiping cloth
horizontally on his fingertips
as he steps back from a reborn white Volvo.

And now it's *déjà vu*
on this bursting
California spring
day, and he's a crimson-and gold-robed monk
spinning his prayer wheel
high in a mountain meadow among
disappearing patches of snow.
I can hear it whir in my ear
as if a humming bird
were about to plumb for nectar.

Meditating

A cool wind blows
through the iron mountain.

These clouds floating in the inner sky,
of what substance?

The light behind eyelids,
the darkness between crickets' chirpings,

the silence inside and outside the drumbeat,
the melody with its curving, curling tail,

the velvet touch as you sink,
letting go hope, ambition,

dropping below the screen of erotic images
to the sweet source of mother's milk

where *be* and *not be* are fast friends,
to the very rocking, swaying heart of it all,

the oceanic pendulum...and suddenly back again
to the woken world,

where morning light is painting
the white wall white.

II.

Yet Again

I've been behaving as if
I were immortal,
indulging myself,
lazing about, practicing
a divine non-diligence,
as if there were nothing but
endless time
as if I were
a bored god,
a resident of my own
high Olympus,
bunches of purple grapes
on the glass coffee table in
front of me,
the mortals below
seen through passing clouds
engaged in their laughable adventures,
which, nonetheless, I find
myself irresistibly drawn to
and jealously keeping tabs on.

From The Ringing Silence

comes the world, its myriad
manifestations, the ceaseless
changes of the eternal moment—
the sparrows squabbling outside
the window, the refrigerator
humming, the sun rising above
the hills through mottled clouds,
distant hum of traffic,
the pines trees working on their cones,
flowers flowering, apples appling,
my coffee warming down...
No one can keep on top of it all,
no one can control it. We just
let it be, let it unfold,
the ten thousand things pointing
always—if we look—back to the Ultimate,
always right here,
as close as our jugular.

Stalled In The Take-Off Line

I gaze out the window
at a puddle of water at
the edge of the runway.
The wind plays
with its surface,
riffling it back and forth
in a rhythm
my heart knows.
For just an instant
it's clear:
the wind and the water
are making love,
the kind of love
requiring nothing,
a pure giving and taking.
With every ripple
a few dozen
points of light
flicker in and out
of existence.
For a timeless moment,
there is no difference between
appearance and disappearance.

Body Orchestra

Orchestra of skin,
cells, hair, fluids, organs, bones—
I listen to you
late in the stillness of the night
playing out your mysterious song—
steady heart rhythms pulsing anywhere I focus,
counterpoint of filling and emptying lungs.
Forgive my arrogance:
I thought I
was your conductor, self-assured, revered, respected,
waving my baton majestically—
a crescendo here, a little
diminuendo there.
I thought I
was rehearsing you
for some great performance,
failing to notice
after packing the baton away
in its little case
and walking off stage to mad applause,
you my tireless orchestra,
as always, and
for now, played on
without me.

Foot

my whole life
the rhythm

of departure
and return

no sooner pressed to earth
than flying again

my lonely lover
she's always leaving

just as I return
returning just as I leave

we serve something higher,
we think, obscured in clouds

we wonder about this
in the still times

side by side
nuzzling the earth

or late at night balanced
on our heels, toes

probing the dark

Well, Poetry Man

where are the poems, the words
dripping with light, sprung from your word horde
like doves out of the magician's black sack?

Well, Poetry Man, where are the metaphors,
the comparisons between ravens and spanners,
between doldrums and dotage, between the Sargasso Sea
and the psyche of a schizophrenic?

Where be the images,
the synesthesia of loud purples
smelling their way along the spinning Dharma Wheel?

Where be the rhythms, syncopated and non-,
the iambs and trochees, anapests and dactyls,
where be the thumping and subtle rhythms of a heart-felt poem?
where is the light that illumes not only dazzles?

Ah Poetry Man, poetry, man...

Legs

Hold him up there!
Keep him steady!
Whoa, don't let him fall.
OK, it's under control.
He wants to go, come on,
forward march, let's go,
left right, left right.
Slow it down; he's seen something.
Whoa! Stop!
Keep him steady, keep him steady.
Let's go, he wants off again.
Uh oh, he wants speed,
pick 'em up, pick 'em up,
put 'em down, ours
not to reason why, etc.
Keep it going. More glucose, goddamnit!
Send us more glucose!
Hang in there Calves, Quads,
he can't keep this up forever.
OK, OK, slow it down,
hold it, steady, steady.
Sonofabitch, he wants to kneel.
Right here, right now.
OK, OK, come on Knees,
do your stuff.

Writing Before Writing

I am four years old
and I sit at the kitchen table, legs a-dangle.
I grip Father's Very Important Fountain Pen
with my fingers awkwardly. It is big,
blue, what I later learn is known as tortoise shell.
Its gold nib and cap's gold clip gleam
with the mysterious wealth of old Europe.

I write across white paper,
wavy, loopy, zig-zaggy lines
scrolling from left to right
just like my father's writing
but embellished with spatters and blots.

I think I know I'm not writing
recognizable words or letters, just as I know
I have not learned the alphabet.
My scrawling is some proto-form of script
crawling right-ward across the page,
searching for some yet-to-be determined meaning,
my four-year-old's attempt
at leaping into the world with words.

Santa Ana

For hours the wind performed
its separations—leaves
off trees, shingles off rooves, hats
off heads, did a better job even
than language itself.
The Santa Ana
rearranged the world.
Oh, I would rearrange the world as well:
beyond the exchange of dead
leaves from yard to yard, beyond
the neighborly fence, its rotted posts
snapped, lying derelict
in its failure, fence no more—
kindling, embers, ash.

A Poem Instead of Excercise

This afternoon I skip
the aerobics class.
I'd rather sit here
and leaf through
Rainer Maria Rilke's
"Sonnets to Orpheus"
in awe of a sensibility
wholly unlike my own.
Rilke, you old Germanic
word monger,
syntax mangler,
hertz-singer.
I wonder
how you'd do
in my aerobics class,
half-jacking,
knee-lifting,
up-sitting
among women
in buttocks-cupping
yoga pants. There's
your maiden in the ear,
there's your
inspirational Euridyce!

Shell

Who will protect me
who protects the soft and unborn?

I'm between you
and all you fear—what skin burnt
once too often becomes.

Who will keep me who remains
after the born have departed
into the world, that place of hard edges,

when I have become one of those hard
edges, shadow of a memory
of softness curving inside?

Among Eucalyptus Trees
—for Peter Skrzynecki

I'm sitting at a desk on the fourth floor of the University of California Library in San Diego in a grove of eucalyptus trees on the shores of the Pacific Ocean listening to a tape of a dead man reading his poetry. At the next desk sits Peter, someone I haven't seen for twenty-two years, a boyhood friend visiting from Sydney where we both grew up among eucalyptus trees and doctrines of the Blessed Virgin Mary. The voice through the earphones is Robert Lowell's saying something about the Hudson River, the river of fourteen years ago, not the same river you and I can step in now. I close my eyes and let the images I carry of New York, Jersey and the Hudson surface, and I don't know whether they resemble anything Lowell saw, but I hear the sadness in his voice, the restraint, the catch in the throat, and I know it's all my own, too. I hear the words, their rhythm and movement, the words pointing darkly, sometimes joyfully beyond themselves. I open my eyes. Through the huge plate-glass windows of the library the tops of the eucalyptus trees wave gently back and forth in exactly the same rhythm as the trees that lulled me to sleep in my childhood in Australia. In one of those sudden perceptual shifts I see the reflection of my friend and myself beyond the window pane, suspended ghostlike, holographic among the branches of the timeless trees.

A Close Call

As I walked outside after class,
a huge branch from the tall eucalyptus tree, fell
right in front of me.
It was astonishing!
The branch—or something in the tree—
had made a sharp crack followed by a rustle,
so that I thought someone
was in the tree trimming
(how quickly simple phenomena become stories),
and I flashed on a boyhood memory
of playing among branches
and seemed to smell again
with an innocent boy's nose
that heavenly smell of being in a tree
among its leaves, its bark, its uncompromised being,
a witness to the ordinary ground below—
and then a thunderous explosion
as the branch simply de-parted
from the rest of the tree and fell,
plummeted, actually, to the ground
just ahead of me
on the path I was walking,
and I heard myself, as though I heard
a stranger, whisper, "Marvelous!" in that split second
before fear arrived, sirens wailing.
The only other witness, a woman
approaching from the distance, face pale,
gasped, "That branch could have landed on you!"
"Yes," I said, "Yes, I know; it could have,"
though I also knew in my heart
for just a second that
"coulds, shoulds, and woulds"
have no being in the world of trees and branches,
nor even in the world of teachers and poets
just recently out of class.

Jury Pool

Down from the local hills
two hundred of us have cascaded
and pooled together in this dank
swamp of a room, exchanging humid gases.

We wait for the summons from above,
wait for the exalted cloud chamber of His Honor's
courtroom to call us.

We're a current pool of somewhat
Patriotic Americans (so the introductory film
has told us), a breathing, mumbling,
computer-key clicking, message-texting,
sometime social-exchanging
granfaloon of prospective moral arbiters
who will rely on our
native "common sense"
to damn the guilty and save the innocent
thereby upholding the grand vision of
the Constitution and Bill of Rights.

But time passes slowly, here in the Jury Pool...
Crossword grids fill up, pages flip,
feet jiggle, heads nod forward
as we wait for The Law to choose us
or not...And some are alphabetically summoned
and float up and out of this room
to the higher chambers above
while the rest of us break for lunch, coffee, bathrooms.
The day wears on and in the soporific room
we are given the call to go home, released
to the wider world at last, free at last
of all but our own judgments.

Four Recurring Dreams

The Neglected

The feeling always of an exquisitely painful
shock of recognition—followed by great relief:
the glowing aquarium

into which I've dropped no food
in what seems like a millennium, still holds
its two fish nonetheless, floating, serenely alert,

their regal, soulful eyes regarding me;
the chickencoop in the backyard, three
new generations of chickens among

the tangled weeds, also unfed, but
miraculously unharmed, scratching in the dirt,
preening bright feathers; that mysterious garden, lush

with vegetables and fruit, ladybirds and aphids.
How could I have forgotten to water
it for so long? How could I have forgotten

its very existence? Though I know I'm supposed to,
I have not fed any of these little creatures
of the dream world, these fish

and fowl, this flourishing vegetation. And yet
something has sustained them—more
than sustained them—allowed them to thrive,

secretly and continuously, away
from the day's fadings and disappointments, beyond
any arrogant husbandry.

The Motorcycles

Freud and Jung would make much of my motorcycles,
these alternating dreams of frustration and power:

desperately wringing the throttle on the handlebar,
the bike putt-putting feebly down some dark street,

me late for an appointment somewhere. Or,
this hog between my legs, thrusting me forward

toward some bright future, redolent
with promise and mystery.

The Basketball Game

It's the old high-school gang—
or sometimes the Lakers—
and the action is furious.

Usually something's wrong with the ball.
It's too big or too small or won't bounce properly, or
when I shoot my arms feel too heavy and the ball arcs
and falls pitifully short.

Once in a while, the game goes well.
I'm all over the court, turning jump shots, spinning lay-ups, off-
balance hooks, all cleanly swishing the net, me
weightless and with no other life anywhere.

Skiing

more than skiing—flying

down impossible

slopes,

eighty-nine degrees

steep   over

crevasses and across

gulches,

in deep snow

and across patches of open ground

swinging

the only word for it

back and forth

like some

archetypal

pendulum

of speed.

A Domestic Love Poem
  —for Arlie

I like attics,
the possibilities for transcendence.
You prefer cellars,
the underness of things.
Say, someday, I float off;
say, you drop through the bottom.
In the meantime, say
we just dance on the pitching floor
of the living room.

Incident

As I sat at my desk one early morning,
a dove flew full force into the plate-glass door.
The thump, like a small bomb exploding,
shocked me and round I spun
to see her on the ground outside,
neck twisted, beak apart, eyelid slowly lowering,
in her death throes, a delicate
shudder, beak closing one last time,
and then a stillness of feathers,
beautiful feathers,
one-of-a-kind,
never-to-be-grown-again
feathers.

A Dream Friend
—for Federico Moramarco

Federico shows up just as he was in life,
vital and ebullient, ready
to cook something Italian and *delicioso*,
pouring us, his friends, large goblets of *Valpolicello*
as we gather yet again to celebrate something
under his welcoming roof.

In the dream, I love him as I did in life,
but minus that mean
tendency I had to needle him
whenever he'd wax pontifical
(I'm Italian, he'd say, I have a special dispensation to pontificate).
But now, he's a distilled Federico,
nothing but lucid, large-souled generosity.

Speaking of lucid, let's forget about
lucid dreaming, seeing through the dream,
waking there suddenly,
perhaps taking up the invitation to manipulate
its content for more pleasure, say
Dream Federico and Dream Al hooking
up with a couple of Dream Babes.

Yes, yes, of course, let us
awaken some day to this ordinary life
to its inarguable joy and pain,
but in this state, let me sleep and dream
of the departed as they return
free of life's bursting suitcases and
none the worse for wearing death,
all smiles, their arms wide open,
offering their impossible and heart-breaking
gift of presence.

The Guilty Tree

that had wantonly raised itself up
on the center divide of our street—
a Canary Island Pine—has been sawed
down, reduced to a stump,
an inadvertent coffee table
oddly in the middle of the street
in the middle of our lives,
upon which has been placed
a vase of cut flowers,
and next to which someone
has planted a white plastic cross.

We all hope the tree has learned its lesson:
that will teach it to wave its branches
seductively in the breeze, attracting
those lascivious starlings and mockingbirds,
enticing drivers to mount the curb
for one last wild
and drunken embrace.

Migrant Hostels
(Bonegilla, Uranquinty, 1949)

Without carte blanche access
to the Akashic Record only
fragments remain: children
building toy boats from wood scraps,
my father under a tree by a creek bank
singing a sad Lithuanian folk song,
long walks with my mother in the countryside,
a train whistle from afar and in my heart at the same time,
the strange unpalatable food,
the hours of the day, the days gone
nowhere to be found.
Who were we then
and what are we now?

Twilight Ruminations At Land's End
Birdrock, California

1.
June 7

How many times have we sat by the sea at twilight,
or noon, or in the morning, and listened while
the waves gnawed at the coast, chewing on pebbles,
masticating them into grains of sand,
those grains into grains too small for the naked eye,
ground into molecules, atoms, quarks.
No wonder the early Greeks came up with the atomic theory,
living by the sea and sifting the white sand through
their ancient fingers.
It took the Buddha, though,
to reduce the atomic particle to the essential
groundless ground of nil, nada, nothingness,
emptiness.
How many times
have we listened as the jets passed high overhead
burning fossil fuels, spraying the earth
with their refined, transformed leavings of leavings.
We've sat and watched the sunlight
play off the waves, the wrinkled sea surface,
ever-changing, ever the same, the colors now a silvery green,
translucent under wave peaks where lowering sun shines through.
We've sat and watched the joggers exercising their
hearts and lungs, have been those joggers...

Forget this childish angst,
away with all dissatisfaction,
begone nostalgia for the never-was,
the never-to-be.
I forego all past regrets, all
future worries.
I take pen to paper

put down my thoughts, whatever they are,
(who will care, anyway?)
I put them down, waiting
for the images to come, to
bubble up (even so, the clichés
usually first in line—I reject them not at all,
I'm Whitmanesque in my global acceptance,
my soul's largeness). That wave curling
and spraying foam into the coming evening,
I count it a gift and a blessing, just as
the cyclist whirring by on rolling
snake's lungs of rubber is a gift,
though a strange one, and,
of course, that dark-haired beauty
with her crone grandmother/auntie/friend,
both of them chewing their evening meal together
on a bench by the Pacific at high tide twi-lit
late twentieth century California
unaware they are being entered into this poem
and celebrated and praised even as the sun
lowers, micro-degree by micro-degree visibly
and birds and boats pass by, cars pass by,
the mist beginning to roll in on its swirling
coils of grey snakes' ghost-lungs.
My dark-haired beauty
now folds up a black and white checkered
tablecloth, puts it away into a wicker
picnic basket. She takes her crone
grandmother/auntie/friend by the arm
and they shuffle to the edge of the cliff,
the edge of America (I know that's what they're thinking),
face out into the ocean, my young beauty
now speaking loudly in is it Vietnamese?
They turn and come back along the cliff
pausing, as if listening, by some yellow,
silently trumpeting flowers.
They love each other, the care-taker

and the care-taken, treading softly
on gravel in those soft black canvas shoes
seen on the feet of people doing Tai Chi
in China on misty mornings.
And now my beauty has unlocked
a car door with keys that dangle and sparkle
in the slanting light
and the door muffles shut, a motor starts
(Oh sacred little sound of my soon-to-be-gone twentieth century,
not heard by Plato though he would claim
already there in ideal, soundless form),
and they're gone
rolling away on the black anaconda lungs
of their tires...

2.
June 14

...same sea?
If you can't step into the same river
twice surely you can't look at the same ocean
more than once, and once becomes once
forever and never.
This evening so different from last week's—
cool and windy, leaden clouds (remember
I'm of a mind to accept my first thought, cliché
though it be); well, ok, clouds dark and heavy
like the underside of giant root vegetables.
No one here today, no humans, just
waves, birds, flowers.
A string of five pelicans skim by
inches above the water, an organized squadron
as it seems to me, the leader cutting the air
with wing beats, the followers gliding, still-winged
in their leader's roiled up currents.
To the left of the land-and-seascape I'm in,
another two pelicans float on the water, ruffling

their feather with long beaks,
together they make one mysterious pair of chopsticks
nervously picking at food.
In my short-sleeved shirt I'm cold.
Are the pelicans cold, if so,
cold in the same way I am?
I suspect yes, but can we ever know for sure?
A whale wind vane, flukes raised, swings
back and forth in the shifting wind, someone's image
of something from the magnificent depths,
something of the human and mammalian
infused into the beaten metal,
itself smelted from the earth.
Across the inlet, a human being
in the lower right of my living land-and-seascape—
and a dog, at this distance neither's gender apparent.
Oh, generic human and representative canine,
at this distance, I can easily love you both, forgive
you your indiscretions and peccadillos
which I can't see from here but can easily imagine.
Excuse me, Canine, not you, you're
indiscretion free...though, again, how
can I be sure. Perhaps in your canine world
you live by some template of rules?
Yes, I've seen it in your eyes, your
soft and warm liquid eyes, your fiercely protective eyes,
your mobile, emotional eyebrows, your cowering,
human-pleasing-mandated body that can
make me ache with love and pity...

3.
June 20

In the foreground, silently trumpeting flowers—
What are they, nasturtiums?—
have truly grown silent, the silence
of bent over and withered defeat.

In the midground/midwater the waves line up,
proceeding toward the shore.
And what is it that proceeds?
Energy, not even water which in the wave merely
goes up and down, eternal aquatic yo-yo.
So, I, a human, containing a few dollars' worth of highschool lab
chemicals
and the whole of the Universe, sit
in a changing land-and-seascape and perceive
the illusion of something coming toward me
while the reality dances and swings up
and down, back and forth
and I do too, and I do, too.

4.
July 26

Sun slants in low, under-lighting the clouds.
Sheets of bright reflection play on the sea's
surface twenty miles out.
Close in, low-tide-exposed rocks and people wandering on them.
A kayaker and surfer dancing with the waves.
A gull rides the updraft along the shore,
passes overhead, head turning side to side, bright
eye considering my half-finished bean and cheese burrito.
Sitting on the cliff, a half-dozen human sunset watchers
grow suddenly still, drop instantly into a trance
as the glowing orange orb of the sun
touches the dark line of the horizon,
and then visibly sinks, second by precious second, or
more accurately, disappears as our planet spins away
from the sun at a thousand miles per hour.
For us, though, all is silence and stillness
as day yet again becomes night
and we're left with the irreducible
fact of the passing of our lives
and the irreducible fact of the wonder of the sun,
the sea, the birds, and our own mysterious place in it all.

III.

A Grain Of Salt

True, the map is not
the territory, the menu not
the meal, the itinerary not
the journey, and the word not

the thing, but even
the thing—*das Ding*—is not
the thing. Ain't no
such thing as a *thing*.

So when we pass the salt
we pass the Universe.
Tasting the salt, we swallow
the seven seas.

Two American Poets In Almost Identical Vests
—for Stephen Dunn

In the snapshot, the two side-by-side poets
are laughing, faces flushed with wine
and the fellowship of being together again
after a long time and having found each other
to be the proud owners of identical red vests
and discovering that each uses his vest
exclusively for poetry readings,
and so the wife of one of them
is prevailed upon to take
this historic snapshot of the two of them,
the two Contemporary American Poets
in their identical red poet vests,
and now, looking closely,
we see the vests are identical in style
but the details of pattern
are dispersed differently around the respective garments,
the one poet having the electric-blue paisley fishy-looking design
closer to his right breast, the other poet
having his under the left breast, and the brightly
speckled yellow flowers are growing
in different parts of the two vest-fields,
and, look, we see the one poet's vest
has five buttons, the other's only three!
and it's true that the three-button poet
probably used his vest more frequently,
hence losing the two buttons somewhere
together or separately
on the Contemporary American Poetry Scene,
and the five-button poet
has survived his fewer readings, buttons intact.
Ah, these two poets with their differing
quotients of fame! But, looking even more closely,
we see that the "missing" buttons on the one

vest are, after all, not missing, just
tilted slightly away from the camera's flash
and so less visible. The two poets' vests
are restored to their provisional identity,
and our previous theory of the poets'
respective fames must now be modified
to include the idea that the more famous of the two poets
has also survived his fame with all five buttons!
We must leave them now
with their bright, almost glowing vests,
that serve no real function,
are pure expression of delight
or so-called male adornment,
two almost identical and separate vests
made in India, purchased in the United States
East coast and West coast
but perhaps after all
cut from the same cloth with threads
that go back to Emerson and Thoreau, Whitman
and Dickinson, Tagore, Basho, Ovid, Sappho, Du Fu
and Li Bai—and let's not forget the paisley design
named after Lord Paisley who first saw it in India,
the design, it turned out later, modelled
on certain microscopic critters
and such design used on Indian clothes centuries
before the invention of the microscope,
our poets, then, in the ancient and true tradition
of noting and describing what's there
before the rest of us have eyes to see it.

Raven Sits

on garbage can
figuring out
how to get a meal without
committing to the possibly flawed
plan of just hopping in

glint of black eye
ruffle of blue-sheen feathers
and wise bird he settles for
a scrap of detritus
on the concrete sidewalk below

where the wingless
two-leggeds stagger along
ice-cream cones
and coffee cups in hand

ort in beak
he beats his black feathered
shoulders and climbs the air
as easily as a human
raises cup to lip

Sputnik

I was twelve when they launched it. *The Daily Mirror* said it would pass over Sydney around two in the morning on a certain night. My father, with his well-developed sense of history, suggested we all get up and witness its flight overhead.

My mother and sister decided they could live without honoring the occasion, and so my father gently woke me just before two, and we went out into the backyard to wait for the quintessential manifestation of twentieth century technology to appear before our naked eyes.

Many years later now, writing this in Southern California under the occluded stratosphere, I remember the night sky above Sydney as clear and immense, moonless but filled with uncountable stars, their light alone clarifying the silence.

We waited, craning our necks upward, to catch the only forward movement in the pulsing night sky.

Under the bathing light of the stars our backyard lay transformed: the rotary clothesline like some astral antenna, the wire-mesh fence around the chicken coop, the vegetable garden breathing in the luminous night engaged in its secret exchanges.

We waited, lost for a while in our own small Dreamtime, and then my father spotted it, cutting in a straight line right through the glowing dust of the Milky Way, through the entangled constellations. It moved with an unhurried, almost arrogant, purpose.

I followed it as it passed directly above, my head back, mouth wide open, followed it for some time, eyes focused on the steady point of human light, as it modified the Southern Cross—momentarily and forever.

Infinite Mouse Courage

Now I know
how it is that Terrytoons
created Mighty Mouse

and Sylvester the Putty Tat.

Rounding the corner of my house,
I see the tiny field mouse
turn at last and rear up on hind legs
tinier paws up
like a cornered boxer
and face the monster cat.

Oh, what courage
to turn and face
your doom, even as its maw
widens above you.

The Preposition Poem

he said he was down
they had passed him by
left him behind
he said he was through
what was it all about
anyway he was so low he was below
he was past pissed off
and was surely tired of being screwed with
screwed over
in short he was really fucked up
to say the least was not beside
himself with joy between
you and me and that fly on
the wall he's another victim of
prepositional anxiety, out of
which it's very hard to get out of
which well you know what I mean by
all means they just don't let you up
once they've got you down
they'll only mess you up
they're bound to put you down
and sometimes out
they'll put you under
for sure down
and dirty they'll get you in
the end the behind
run you through
your only hope is to go out
way out
beyond the back of beyond
for that you've got to be out
of here out of
it you can't continue to screw around
with it you gotta take it up

and over
over and out
that is if you really get down
and if you really know what's going down
which is to say you know what's up
at least which end's up
and then you can go down
whether to the river or on
a close friend or spouse they'll get you off
and then you'll be right on
that's what its all about
Alfie, that's what it's all about,
love sweet love that's the only thing I'm thinkin' of

Poem About A Friend's Archetypal Experience
—for Philip Dacey

He was sitting by a river on a rock contemplating the mystery of the moving water-that-is-always-there. He was in his bathing suit, having just come out of swimming in a spring-fed pool. His wife and two fair sons were walking in the extreme left-field of his vision. His heart warmed toward them even as he continued to puzzle over the moving-water-that-is-always-there. He wondered what it was like to be a fish in the river, a fish without hands, without glasses, without a job teaching creative writing. His ribs itched where he imagined his fins would be. He loved the mystery of the moving-water-that-is-always-there as he sat on the rock with his legs spread like a woman ready for love. And so, on that day, he was given a gift out of the Garden itself: from under the rock under his crotch a small green snake wound itself out, raised its head (which was not ugly) and not realizing it was playing a major role in a minor archetypal event, slid off down the garden path. My friend, understandably moved by this experience, told me about it in the locker room as we changed for racquetball. I made up all the stuff about the moving-water.

In Praise of Fashion

Let us praise them,
these goddesses gliding in and out of
the coffee house this summer morning,

these Lakshmis and Parvartis,
toe-rings a-jingle,
draped in celestial fabrics,

floating on shoes and sandals
better made for treading clouds.
And the gods, too: that Adonis

with the glowing orange
skin-tight tank and matching Nikes,
biceps and calves worthy of Hercules...

and the shoulder tattoo of, what,
a verse from *Revelations?*
Even the little children, the cherubs

with their gauzy, pink frills,
that little chap in the Spiderman
outfit, months ahead of Halloween...

Everyone is decked out
asking to be seen,
begging for the benedictive beholder's eye,

to be seen, and seen some more,
and we, lookers all, voyeurs even,
we gaze, regard, stare, and look again,

all of us insatiable for something
we can never name but recognize,
in the beautiful fleeting forms.

Before The Piano Lesson

Mrs. Reidl, my old Austrian piano teacher,
would take me through the same ritual
each time I arrived for my lesson:
In the bathroom, she'd watch
while I washed my hands
and scrubbed my fingertips
with the soap-stone she kept for her pupils.
When I dried my hands, she'd hold them
to the light, scrutinize them for deeply
engrained finger-print grime,
and only if my fingertips were as pink and clean
as new-born mice would she lead me back
to her small room full of doilies
and the dry must of faded and neat
pages of classical sheet music,
the room of her lonely immigrant widowhood
and its ancient piano.
Raising the waxed, funereal lid,
she'd wipe the yellowed keys with a green velvet cloth,
check my posture, the position
of my hands and feet, put up the music—
all those wonderful pieces by
Mozart, Beethoven, Schumann
which I always failed to
ever play cleanly enough.

At The Memory Care Facility
—for my mother, Ona Smilgevicius Zolynas

The old folks
show up by ones and twos,
file into the room for Morning Stretch,
shuffling, leaning on canes and walkers, assisted
by aides and nurses.
They're mostly quiet, though Cathy and Meg,
apparently the resident cut-ups,
chortle and elbow each other as they settle
side by side into high-backed chairs.

Becky, the young exercise leader, comes in,
brisk and happy, young and beautiful.
She engages them in banter; it's clear they love her.
She takes them through the motions—
stretching, flexing wrists and ankles,
raising arms, kicking legs.
Some follow along,
others sit as still as Buddhas.
They are deep in the mysterious
meditation of dementia.
One sleeps lolled over in her chair.

One of the resident dogs trots in, appraises all
with intelligent yellow eyes, accepts a few fondles
behind the ears and leaves.

After some Sit and Stay Fit, we move
to Exercises for the Brain.
Meg says she's lost hers. Becky says,
No, don't worry, we'll dig it out
and begins with A, asking for words
that start with A.
Slowly we build a list—*Arizona...Arkansas...*

apple...action...ask...
and from my mother beside me...*Anton...*
which causes Becky the leader to say
Ona, could you repeat that please?
I jump in for my mother, spelling it out.
Becky, I can tell, has never heard that name.
How could she, a name from Eastern Europe,
from two generations ago, the name
of one of my parents' dearest friends,
long gone from this Vale of Tears, as my
father used to say before
he departed the Vale himself.

We finish a flip-chart page's worth of *B*'s
and it's time for Sing-Along,
while Becky goes off
to prepare a Sweet Treat for everyone.
We follow along in the songbook
as a woman accompanied by a piano on a CD sings
the old songs in a voice that makes
me lower my head and squeeze back tears.
I notice one of the deep meditators
is back with us now mouthing the words
of a song she must have known in her girlhood.
I sing along a little, too—*Daisy Daisy, A Bicycle Built
For Two, Irene Goodnight...*

A different dog wanders in, a small
longhaired black and white
Chihuahua who jumps in my lap until
the treats arrive, two small pieces each of
yellow pound cake. Everyone eats
slowly, attentively. No one is in a hurry,
no one has anywhere they need to go.
Becky hand feeds a piece of cake
to the woman on my right, a quiet,
dignified Asian lady, still as a daguerreotype.

She barely remembers how to open her
mouth and chew.

And now, as always, it's time
for the next thing, time for the residents
to return to their rooms where
they will re-check their meager closets,
their small treasures,
take a nap before lunch.
And it hits me like the most obvious revelation,
the most ordinary epiphany:
the old folks are not yet dead;
they have a life they are actually
living right now, even here, so far
removed from all they used to know.
They're surrounded by care and even love
in the midst of their sufferings.
They bear those sufferings
with patience and acceptance.
If my life comes to this, will
I be able to as well?...
Will I, too, be able to take this life
just as it's given, just as it always is?

The Neighborhood Egret

An egret has come to live in our neighborhood
in the small green sward at the foot of our street,
a wild white creature, eternal in her presence,

among the impermanence of our suburban homes,
among our domesticated cats and dogs.
She daily walks the mown grass, mostly stills herself into

a glowing alabaster sculpture above her
unsuspecting prey of insects and frogs.
Driving to and from work, I see her almost every day.

How she lifts my spirits, gladdens and saddens me all at once
with her pure life among us wingless two-leggeds.
The other day, walking, I looked up and

saw her gliding prehistorically down the slope,
her long yellow bill, her forward-curved
neck, archetype for all ship-prows...and with a back-beat

of wings, she landed on her yellow stilts, adjusted
her shoulders and began again her stop
and go dignified pacing of the meadow.

Fragment: The Good Life, Southern California Style

She's one of those young
upper-middle class, suburban mothers,
healthy, athletic, who has set herself up
for a late morning break
outside the local Starbucks
with her non-blue and non-pink clad toddler
whose gender is, therefore, impossible
to tell in these politically correct times,
and her Golden Retriever.
Both child and canine are tethered, leashed
to the wrought iron chair, and both
explore the ground under the table
while Mom sips her iced mocha latte, gently
breaks her pound cake and inserts tiny pieces
one at a time into her mouth.
From the recesses
of her three-wheeled baby carriage
she magically produces
a clear plastic doggie bowl and fills
it up with designer water.
The Retriever gratefully slurps it up
on this warm spring day.
It seems, two other mothers and
their bright-eyed toddlers
join her at the table.
They've all been jogging,
have pushed their baby carriages up
and down these considerable suburban hills.
Now they sit around laughing,
legs crossed, Nikes and Reeboks tapping away
under the table as the caffeine level rises.
I'm just far enough away
to not hear their words.

Re-Call Of The Wild
(2020-21, The Pandemic)

The Virus, that miniscule sentience
lurking in submicroscopic caves,
ventured out to find welcome
in human inspiration.

Then the larger visible ones
began encroaching across
suburban borders—
fences, walls—seemingly
abandoned by us, no longer
holding their trespass threats.

Small country roads and paths
became permitted ways for deer,
coyote, cougars
to reclaim their losses.
Why tread down long grass, bend
back brush and thicket
when smooth black pavement,
gentle to hooves and paw pads,
showed the way?

From trees and rooftops new songs
(they felt louder) greeted us
in the morning. We saw more
hawks and vultures spiral slowly
up the invisible air columns
above our houses.

In the night owls drew closer
and hooted to us in our sleep.
We still didn't know what they said
but we liked that they felt
comfortable saying it closer.

A fraught time for some of our pets
who smelled the air through screen doors
for whatever lingered
after the coyote left the yard.

Oh, over wine at dinner
we celebrated the Return of Nature.
We rejoiced in what we hoped
would be a turn favorable to Gaia,
to a cleansing of the seas,
a scrubbing of the air.

We put a positive spin on the Virus
and the lockdown—
until the next surge
and the crowding of the ICUs,
until it became clearer still that
the re-call of the wild
included not only the furry and feathered ones,
the scaled and shelled,
but the tiny Virus itself
with its mysteriously built-in genius
for adaptation, transformation, and
survival.

Life After Work

Missing my go-to job, my daily
workmates, I may be turning into one of those old
codgers who must pass the time of day with every
waiter, barista, and check-out girl
he comes across during a day's suburban foraging.

How easy—and difficult—to connect.
Easy if you accept a little eye contact, a friendly word, or the gesture
that says, "Oh, well, yes, ain't it strange
and funny and sad that we're in this—
whatever this is—all together,
here and now," and a little more difficult
when the platitudes run out but
the need to connect is still sitting
there like an unopened envelope.

I must guard my searching eye as it peers in;
some folks seem wary of the empty head behind
these unemployed eyeballs.

After all, I have "nowhere to go, nothing to do"
beyond maintaining a few basic needs and desires,
like working on my own rapidly fading
literary ambitions, and keeping an aging body marginally
in shape for as long as possible
(current activity: racquetball with other aging boomers).

With my grey hair and everyone "sir-ing" me left and right,
deferring to what they see as
my venerable age, respecting,
pitying, discounting, ignoring, or simply not seeing me—it's a trip.
I tell you, this sallying out into the world every day
with no more Gainful Employment than the tasks
I assign myself—or the ones assigned by
Madame Necessity, ruler of us all.

Something of the blessed innocence of boyhood about it all,
though my pale blue bicycle has long rusted back into the earth,
and the Bush I explored with its goannas and frilly-necked lizards and
waratahs has fallen to the newer suburbs...No more
morning bells, teachers, sums, civics lessons,
history of the glories of the Empire...
just an old man with a boy's heart
out on his daily ventures and errands, not Ulysses-like at all,
not chest out, shoulders back, bearded chin sprayed by sea spume,
strapped to the mast against the Sirens' call,
ever seeking some epic adventure, some mega over-existence.
No, not at all, more like the astonishing blessedness
of an ordinary day with its apples and coffee and car radio.

A Project, In Process

The late winter Santa Ana blew
through here, combed clean the last
dry leaves from neighborhood trees
and dropped a long, gnarled branch from
the maple in our front yard.

When I stooped to move it, something
in its shape spoke to me:
"Trim me up a bit," it said,
"and you'll have a good walking stick
for your old age, your doddering years."

Shocked, I picked it up, found
a rusted saw, and made two
quick cuts through the ends of the wood.
There was my crude walking stick,
gnarly still but almost useful,
though still bristling branchlets along its shaft.

The branch-Ur-stick's voice grew in
confidence: "Get your father's knife, the one
he carried all the way from the old country,
and lop off those branchlets, and
scrape off some bark. Later,
you can sand and rub me down—maybe with
linseed oil, like your old man showed
you all those years ago
with your first cricket bat.
Later still, you can screw an iron ferrule
on to the end to tap your way down
the rough sidewalks, the long halls of
your coming agedness.
Oh, you'll be doddering in style someday, you will!"

EPILOGUE
Months later, the drying branch leans against
the garage wall, most of its bark scraped off
but still unfinished, a Walking Stick
in imagination only.
It waits, sometimes whispers
as I walk by on the way
to the garbage can or to get the day's mail,
something about finishing what I started,
something about getting ready.

New Car

In this short life, probably more
than an auto-maker's dozen.
Those shifting forms of
metal and plastic,
the increasingly sonorous
alarms and bells,
the palpable sense of something
large and uncontrollable
taking over,
keeping us in our lanes,
guarding our blind spots.

The Unthinkable

How could it be? After all, he'd been a fabled
lover, bon vivant, everyone's party animal,
raconteur, matinee idol, rock star, father
of the year, deep Zen meditator, Big Wave surfer.
He'd been an All Round Good Sort, the very model
of a Perfect English Christian Gentleman,
a friend to the downtrodden, a champion
of everyone's civil rights—
indeed, a Bodhisattva, a Kosmic-centered
Dude of all Dudes.

And yet, now, it must be said plainly,
he was the Old Codger, alone in a backwoods trailer
with his old hound and crusted coffee pot; or
the retired banker, tethered to his penthouse suite by
a plastic oxygen tube; or
the Alzheimer's inmate, reporting over and over to
the generic ghost office down the hall
with its sheets of blank papers, blank folders,
staple-less staplers in the desk drawers,
set up by the caretakers to mimic
that powerful life once lived and left behind,
to offer solace and security,
so too the continuous hallway
that squared the facility in the simplest but,
to him, most unfathomable maze
that always brought him back to where he'd started,
though where that was he no longer knew.

Stilts

Once my father made me
a pair of stilts, the envy of everyone
on Petunia Avenue. I became
an expert at hobbling around,
could even perform
grotesque versions of running,
hopping, skipping.

Soon, stilts appeared
up and down the block.
Georgie, next door, built a pair
that shot him up
well over six feet,
and his sister—
graceful, athletic Rhonda—
could pirouette
and balance herself impossibly long
on one stilt. I remember

one long summer evening
all of us clumping around
on the pavement in front of my house,
the huge pepper tree across the street
looming over us
full of countless Christmas beetles,
the one street lamp
raining down its benediction
of light
as the sky turned
that particular deep magenta
I've never seen again.

Them Bones

>—for Tony and Jack Gapsis

1

I'm five years old, kicking leaves
with my friend, Patty,
walking through the woods across from her house.
Suddenly, we come upon
the skeleton of a cat on its side
in perfect symmetry.

I remember that shock in my body
(Where did it come from?)
We bent down, squatted to look
closer. Most of the bones
had lost their connections.
I picked up the skull
suddenly reminded
of Patty's father's white Chevrolet
with its sleek curved planes,
its one hollow headlamp-socket, the bright fangs
on both sides.

I threw the skull as far as I could
and we both turned
and tore out of there, terrified
and giggling our heads off.

2.

Diving off the concrete banks
of Lake Michigan in Chicago
the summer after high school graduation,
I found a plain metal container
the size of a cigar box
in about ten feet of water.

I brought it up to show Tony and Jack.
None of us had any idea what it was.
I pried one end open slightly,
tipped it, and black, congealed ashes
dribbled out
and then a human molar.
Again, that shock in the body.

Quickly, I stuffed those violated contents
back into the box, eased into the water,
swam out to where I had found it
and let it sink again.

3.

If I were a visual artist—
a painter or a plastics man—
I'd make a series called
"Bones and Fruit."

They'd be these exquisite renderings:
Say, the human pelvic bone
with a ripe apple miraculously suspended
in the cavity,
or a skull with two purple plums
bulging in the eye-sockets,
or maybe a peeled banana
in a fist of bone,
or even better
two pelvises connected by a banana!

But I wouldn't know
what medium to use.
Should I draw it in charcoal,
paint it in oils?
Should I set it up and photograph it?
Should I make the bones

out of some sort of art-stuff,
mold it out of some special art-clay?
Or why not use real bones?

It's probably good that I don't
carry any of this beyond
the domain of bright ideas
the world can't possibly live without.
I can just see myself
hunting around town for the right kind of bones,
calling up medical schools and hospitals and museums
telling them I'm an artist
and could I please have
some of their spare bones.

It'd be a real test
of my artistic seriousness:
the supermarkets
here in Southern California
bursting with ripe mangoes, papayas, avocados;
another 200,000 dead on the planet today,
and some crazy artist looking
for bones and fruit
and some way to put them together.

Two Old Men On A Bench
—for Spence McWilliams

Two Immortals, they've been sitting
under this Live Oak
for eons, or at least for the last
twenty minutes, resting
from their walk in the noon-day sun.

Are they Han-shan and his friend Shi-teh?
Huck and Jim? Butch and Sundance?

From the tree's shade
they gaze into an arroyo of scrub oak,
manzanita, sage, and
a profusion of California wildflowers
in early Spring bloom.

They converse quietly about
this and that—
old movies they've enjoyed,
Dependent Origination, the identity
of relative and absolute,
and old movies...

What was that one where
oh, old What's-His-Face,
you know, follows Grace Kelly
(or was it Kim Novak) around as she
runs errands in San Francisco?

Cold Mountain, still there.
The Mississippi (Big Muddy), still rolling.
Butch and Sundance suspended
in mid-air above the Animas River
somewhere near Durango.

House Hiking

During the lockdown
we learned
to hike the house,
trekking through
hallway canyons and arroyos,
past sofa mesas and
armchair buttes.
Up and down rip-rap
stairs we labored,
I in bare feet, you in
your trusty hiking slippers.

At the upper story's
thinned-air elevation
we sometimes breached
the French doors
and burst
out onto the sunlit deck
with its wide vista
of a world
we once had known.

About The Author

Al Zolynas is the author of the poetry collections *The New Physics*, *Under Ideal Conditions*, *The Same Air*, *Near and Far*, and *A World Once Known*. He co-edited two poetry anthologies: *Men of Our Time* and *The Poetry of Men's Lives: An International Anthology*. He teaches Zen meditation in Escondido, California where he lives with his wife and their cat.

www.ingramcontent.com/pod-product-compliance
Lightning Source LLC
Chambersburg PA
CBHW031750150726

47989CB00006B/2664